Fargo 1957

Grand prize winner, 11th annual Graflex Photo Contest, "Story of a Tornado."

(Chet Gebert, June 20, 1957)

Fargo 1957

An Elegy by

Jamie Parsley

North Dakota State University Press
Fargo, North Dakota

Also by Jamie Parsley

Paper Doves, Falling and Other Poems (1992)
The Loneliness of Blizzards: poems (1995)
Cloud: A Poem in 2 Acts (1997)
The Wounded Table: prose poems (1999)
earth into earth, water into water (2000)
no stars, no moon (2004)
Ikon: poems (2005)
Just Once: poems (2007)
This Grass: poems (with paintings by Gin Templeton) (2009)
Crow: poems (2012)
That Word: poems (2014)
The Downstairs Tenant and Other Stories (2014)
Only Then: poems (2018)

NDSU NORTH DAKOTA STATE UNIVERSITY PRESS
P.O. Box 6050, Dept. 2360, Fargo, ND 58108-6050
www.ndsupress.org

Second Printing

Printed in the United States of America

International Standard Book Number (ISBN): 978-0-911042-73-3
Library of Congress Control Number: 2010940194

Acknowledgments

First and foremost, very special gratitude and appreciation to my aunt, Shirley Carbno (1934-2011).

Very special thanks to my mother, Joyce Parsley (1936-2018), and to my father, Albert Parsley, who died suddenly and unexpectedly on September 14, 2010, while this book was going into production.

Thanks also to Greg Bachmeier (as usual) and to Sr. Rosaria Acton PBVM (1926-2016), Lynn Brown, John Bye, The Catholic Diocese of Fargo, Ross Collins, Chet Gebert (1927-2013), John Hallberg, Sr. Maris Stella Korb PBVM, Catherine McMullen, Michael J. Olsen, the Sisters of the Presentation of the Blessed Virgin Mary in Fargo, Thomas J. Riley, The Reverend William Sherman, Julia Sorlien, Janet Syrup, Gin Templeton, SuZ Templeton, Dorothy Tronnes (1923-2016), Michael Vosburg, Sr. Maureen Walker PBVM (1930-2013), Leisha Woltjer and the congregation of St. Stephen's Episcopal Church, Fargo.

I am especially indebted to Mark Vinz for his patient editing of these poems and for his many years of friendship. I extend a very big thank you to Suzzanne Kelley of North Dakota State University Press for reprinting this book.

Several of these poems originally were published in the following publications, some in slightly different form: *The Anglican, The Ambassador, The Arts Journal, Arts Pulse, Danse Macabre, The Living Church, Meat for Tea, The Sheaf, The Solitary Plover, The Yellow Bicycle,* and *Writer's Journal.*

In memory:

Betty Lou Olson Titgen and **Donald ElRoy Titgen**
(November 25, 1936 – January 16, 1960) (October 12, 1930 – June 20, 1957)

and

Thedore Udahl
(November 15, 1906 – June 20, 1957)

Theresa Udahl
(May 25, 1917 – June 20, 1957)

Mary Jean Udahl
(October 18, 1948 – June 20, 1957)

Phyliss Munson
(December 2, 1940 – June 20, 1957)

Darwin Munson
(February 28, 1945 – June 20, 1957)

Bradley Munson
(May 16, 1947 – June 20, 1957)

Jeanette Munson
(July 4, 1951 – June 20, 1957)

Lois Munson
(November 22, 1954 – June 20, 1957)

Mary Munson
(February 13, 1956 – June 20, 1957)

Laura Schoenherr
(January 28, 1888 – July 16, 1957)

Maria Sanderson
(March 18, 1908 – February 24, 1964)

Richard Shaw
(June 2, 1936 – August 29, 1969)

Mercedes Munson Erickson
(June 20, 1921 – September 4, 2009)

Contents

II. After the Storm

Afterword: Lux Perpetua

Photo taken by Alf T. Olsen (1920-1970) at the slough on the west side of Fargo, at 11th Avenue and 21st Street South. Among the children in the foreground are Olsen's sons, Patrick and Michael, as well as Terry Farley, and Carol and Barbie Betz. The storm is approaching from the northwest. (NDSU Institute for Regional Studies)

Foreword

It's been a pleasure working as Jamie Parsley's editor, watching the manuscript of *Fargo, 1957* come together, thanks to a great deal of perseverance and hard work on Jamie's part.

This is indeed a book that does many things—weaving together history, religious experience, and a very personal quest, all the while skillfully blending fact, faith, and imagination.

It strikes me, too, that the book has elements of classical tragedy, and with it a tragic catharsis, as the writing itself becomes a kind of resolution and reconciliation. To say the least, *Fargo, 1957* is a labor of vision and of love.

Mark Vinz

Introduction

In the early evening of Thursday, June 20, 1957, a tornado hit the city of Fargo, North Dakota. As it plowed into the city, my mother's cousin, Betty Lou Titgen, and her husband, Don, were lying on the floor of their trailer in the housing development known as Golden Ridge. Don was killed outright, his body found blocks away. Betty was knocked into a coma, from which she never regained consciousness; she died two and a half years later in January of 1960. Nine other people died that day. Another died a month later. One final victim injured in the storm died in 1964 from the lingering effects of those injuries.

I was born twelve and a half years after the tornado. I grew up hearing the story, always in hushed tones, especially whenever the June anniversary drew near or when the summer weather turned dark and the sky threatened tornados. The story of Betty and Don was simply a part of our family history, something that happened, for me, in some other, strangely romantic, slightly halcyon time. I knew few details of the Titgens' deaths and, outside the yearly reminder of it, few members of my family ever talked about it.

Because I was a writer, it was one of those stories that, over time, obsessed me. Over the years, I wrote drafts of poems, short fiction, and even a full-length play about the event, usually to no completed end.

Even as the 50th anniversary of the tornado came and went in the summer of 2007, I felt no real desire to write anything substantial about the event, despite the fact that I followed the commemorative events of that year closely. One year later, however, I suddenly felt overcome by the desire to write the poems in this collection. As I wrote them, I was amazed by how quickly they came forth. Later, as I read through the first draft, it struck me that the poems were strangely, almost eerily familiar. The only explanation

I had for this creative outpouring and the familiarity of the poems was that they had, in fact, existed within me for many years, simply waiting to be written.

As I wrote this book during the hot, stormy summer of 2008, I found myself often driving around the streets of Golden Ridge and north Fargo, passing the approximate locations of the houses (now rebuilt) in which the victims of the tornado lived and died, following the pathway the tornado took through the city.

As an Episcopal priest, I also was fortunate enough to fill in one Sunday that summer for the pastor of Golden Ridge Lutheran Church while he was on vacation. The original building of this church, of which the Udahl family were charter members, was leveled in the tornado. A small stained glass window in the nursery of the rebuilt church shows the tornado bearing down on the original building, and a portrait of Christ that survived the destruction hangs in the vestibule.

I also found myself traveling about North Dakota and Minnesota, searching out the graves of the victims, which only made more real the event and the losses incurred in it. I found graves of victims in Velva, North Dakota (the Udhals); Detroit Lakes, Minnesota (Dick Shaw); Holy Cross Cemetery in north Fargo (Don Titgen); Evergreen Cemetery in south Moorhead, Minnesota (the Munson family); Chaffee, North Dakota (Laura Shoenherr); Sunset Memorial Gardens in Fargo (Maria Sanderson); and Moorhead Memorial Gardens (Betty Titgen). Each victim lay in a simple grave, occasionally decorated with flowers each Memorial Day.

My intention in writing this book was not to present a strictly historical retelling of the events: that project is, I hope, forthcoming and will be left to a historian, not a poet. Rather, this book is meant to be an elegy of sorts. As I researched and interviewed survivors, relatives, and others, I realized this tragic event needed to be commemorated with poetry, if for no one other than myself and my own family members.

Upon completing this book, I feel, in some ways, as though I have finally faced and accepted my obsession with this horrific event. Still, in doing so, I have gained something else as well. These people who died a decade or more before I was even born have become alive for me. Their presence in my life has become real and potent—these were real people, with real hopes and real dreams that were wiped from them on that terrible day. They have also truly become a part of who I am. I have come to realize, through this spiritual bond with them, that there is much truth to the wonderful saying of the thirteenth century German mystic, Mechtild of Magdeburg: "If one blows even on the tiniest spark it brings forth both heat and light in the fire of heaven where all the radiant saints abide."

Jamie Parsley
Fargo North Dakota

Looking southeast toward downtown Fargo from the North Dakota Agricultural College (now NDSU). In the foreground are the ruins of the Agricultural College HastyTasty and the Agricultural College Y.M.C.A. The roofs of both buildings are missing and debris is scattered about. An automobile is visible driving on University Drive North. (NDSU Institute for Regional Studies)

"I will overturn, overturn, overturn, it; and it shall be no more"

— Ezekiel 21.27

(found in an open Bible in the wreckage of American Lutheran Church, Fargo, June 1957)

"It's evident
the art of losing is not too hard to master
though it may look like disaster."

— Elizabeth Bishop

"Don't know where I'm headed for
Makes no difference anymore
Got no future
Got no home
Can't do nothing now but roam."

— "Freight Train" (lyrics by Elizabeth Cotton)
sung by Rusty Draper

(#18 on the Cashbox Top 60 for the week of June 15, 1957)

Plymouth Congregational Church, North Broadway, Fargo. July 7, 1890.

(NDSU Institute for Regional Studies)

Prologue

Monday

July 7, 1890

"O send thy word of command
to rebuke the raging winds..."

— The Book of Common Prayer

McCarty family funeral procession on 6th Avenue North. The Continental Hose Company and Grand Army of the Republic men are in front, followed by horse-drawn hearses and buggies extending into the far distance. Lincoln Elementary School is visible in the background.

(NDSU Institute for Regional Studies)

Terra

The first tornado struck Fargo early in the morning of July 7, 1890. Although the city was heavily damaged, the only deaths were seven children belonging to the recently widowed Rose McCarty, who lived in a house at Ninth Avenue and Fifth Street North. Mrs. McCarty, who was pregnant, survived as did her two other children who happened to be in Hunter, North Dakota, at the time of the storm. One year later, on July 19, 1891, 8-year-old Agnes died from what was thought to be the shock of the loss.

Gone. The last anyone saw of them
was as the gnarled priest
sprinkled blessed water into each open hole,
laid out, side-by-side
before they were filled with children,
washed and cleaned from the coal dust.
They disappeared beneath a tumble
of disturbed sod. What better graves,
everyone thought, than the coal bin
under the collapsed pantry?

Gone
like that. And six hundred people
in unison mourned them
and helped them to their deep trenches.
One by one they let them down.
First, it was Rose Isabella
laid in her place. Next to her, they put
Mary Alice, then Frances Anna,
then James Francis, Justin, Josephine,
and last, in the smallest coffin of all,
Luella.

And when it was done,
there was not a trace left.
Only names inscribed in
a descending pattern
beneath the inscription
JAMES MCCARTY
who died three weeks before
his children.
Seven names
and the mind boggles
when one reaches the bottom
of the stone pillar.

The clerics who stood by during the burying
in their lace cottas
dirty with grave dirt and sawdust
no doubt pondered impermanence as they
gazed into the void, fingering
their breviaries and rosaries. And so it is.
We *are* temporary,
the same way clouds are
when they enter the sky, grow full
as our guts, unleash what they have
and then dissipate. Search as we might,
gazing up with our expectant faces
we find no traces there in the sky we trust in
and ponder ourselves
with the same awe one gives to the divine
mystery after every other solution fails.

We look downward too,
our faces unable to find even one trace of them
except there,
in the overgrown grass
where the white footstones mark
long dents in the earth
and not one thing more.

Maybe they never were, we wonder.
Maybe it's all fantasy,
a tale they tell us when the weather
grows ominous and we shudder
at the first sound of thunder.
It could never happen, we conclude,
not seven of them, gone beneath
the weight of timber and coal.
There's not an ounce of proof anyway—
every footprint, every tear
has been washed into the grass by
some long-ago rain.
All we have are letters
inscribed into pale gray granite,
and the simple curves of the death date.

Maybe, they never were.
Or maybe, they were
and they have in fact
become what we know we are
beneath our uncertain arrogance at death.
Maybe it's true for them
*terra es, terram ibis**
as it is for all of us.

**Earth thou art, and to earth thou shalt return*

The McCarty gravestone, Holy Cross Cemetery, Fargo.
(photo by author)

The tornado forms. Photo taken from the Great Northern Railroad crossing on 19th Avenue North, looking southwest. (NDSU Institute for Regional Studies)

I.
It approaches...

Thursday

June 20, 1957

7:30 p.m.

Fargo, North Dakota

"The view stretches as far as death."

— Edwin Denby

The tornado approaches. Photos taken at the Great Northern Railroad crossing on 19th Avenue North, near Highway 81, looking southwest.
(Dewey Bergquist, WDAY)

Photo looking northeast, with demolished Shanley High School in foreground.
(NDSU Institute for Regional Studies)

Fargo, 1957. (NDSU Institute for Regional Studies)

Golden Ridge, 1957. (NDSU Institute for Regional Studies)

View of storm approaching Fargo taken from 19th Avenue North, near Hector Airport.
(NDSU Institute for Regional Studies)

Flying debris. Photo taken from the campus at NDAC. (NDSU Institute for Regional Studies)

The funnel just west of the NDAC Memorial Union.

(photos NDSU Institute for Regional Studies)

The tornado strikes Fargo. This photo was taken from the roof of the old WDAY building in downtown Fargo. (NDSU Institute for Regional Studies)

From there

"When summer days grow harsh…"
—Judith Wright

My mother:

At twenty, I huddled
in the basement of my house
on the south side of town.
I held my daughter and my infant son

to me and looked up through
the high basement window.
There I saw the air turn green
and thought—

green? have I ever
before
seen the air
turn pea green?

The roar—
the one everyone said was low
like the grumble of a train or a truck—
came then and shook

the floor beneath us.
It was like a freight train
and for days afterward
I shivered every time

I heard Rusty Draper sing
"Freight Train"
on the radio.
My ears popped

and then,
looking up,
I saw boards flying in the air.
My first husband stood

arrogant and barrel-chested,
watching the tall black cloud
weave about,
throwing up wreckage

dirt and trees.
When I called for him to come inside,
my voice cracking
against the sound of the wind,

he ignored me.
Later when the lines were up again,
the phone rang
bringing with its trill the news of my cousin, Betty Lou,

of Betty's husband, Don, whom they found battered
and beyond help.
Days later I donned my hat
and knelt with my sister Shirley at the casket-side,

gazing in stunned silence at the shroud
laid over his battered body.
I listened with the quiet frustration we Lutherans had
at the gibberish the priest intoned

at the altar, his back to us.
And when I came home, my skirt
reeked of incense. I folded
the Fargo *Forum* into thirds,

careful not to crease
the photo of their smiling newly married faces,
and, with a sigh, I set it
in my cedar chest

more gently than
the cemetery workers did,
wrestling and jostling Don's coffin
into its lonely plot

and threw onto it,
without a second thought,
thick, black earth
and heavy clods of sod.

Tornado striking, taken just east of Hector Airport, looking south. (NDSU Institute for Regional Studies)

What more?

My father:

From work
out near Hunter
I raced home
when I saw the cloud heave—

boiling
and roiling
and churning
as it rolled toward Fargo.

My foot jammed to the accelerator, I followed it,
passing cars on the highway,
desperate to get to my first wife,
eight months pregnant.

Outside Mapleton,
I saw the cloud
drop its tail
and when it touched

ground the first time, dirt exploded
as though someone
had stomped a dusty floor
in anger.

I told the story later
the way one tells
tales of blizzards
or the perfect trout.

It happened.
And I did my duty.
I offered to help clean up
the mess, the wreckage

left in a snaking trail
through the north side of town.
And when I was refused,
I shrugged

and walked away.
And that was that.
What more can you do?
What more could anyone do

than go on? What more was there
to do but stand up from
the planks and shattered glass
and wipe the remnants of it from us?

What more could we do but
pick up what was destroyed,
rebuild what was thrown away,
bury what died?

What more
could anyone do
but walk away
and live?

Sirens

My aunt Shirley:

So
we thought that day,
this is what it will sound like!
This is that last
terrible sound.

This is the tune
the angel
will know
on that last unending Day
when he puts the
trumpet to his lips
and blows.
It will sound like sirens,
like a blare that will reach us
no matter where we hide.

We scattered
when we heard that cacophony of wails.
We thought in our stubborn way that we could
escape the wrath
we knew raged just on the edge
of that horizon.

As we drove, we prayed
the only words that came to us
in those moments when words
begin to lose their meaning—
let this not be
the last sound I hear!

Let this not be
what my ears hold onto
as we go up
into the winds.

Every day

Maria Sanderson (1908-1964) was the first person injured by the tornado. She and her husband, Thilford, lived in a house on the western outskirts of Fargo on Highway 10. She died of a stroke (complicated by the injuries she suffered in the tornado) in Minneapolis, Minnesota, on February 24, 1964.

Maria Sanderson
(SuZ Templeton)

Prelude: August 2008

"No one knows
what ghost you feed."
—Joel Oppenheimer

Even with the photocopied township map
printed in 1951, the homestead is nearly impossible to find.
These are streets now, not backroads.
And the highway has become a four-laned artery.

Finally, finding the mile line
and County Drain 40, I can almost make it out.
There, behind a cluster of Quonsets
a line of oak stand, older than
anything else here, older too,
than the storm. And from them,
we can almost see how it was—
a rebuilt house at the end of a gravel driveway
hidden
white walled
between the hulking girth of commercial buildings.

It was here she lived
and it was here she lay that night
after the storm came rolling through
from the northwest.
It was here she struggled
in the wreckage and shattered glass
until Thilford, her husband,
lifted the boards from her
revealing her shattered body.

It's Industrial Park now,
huge metal-walled complexes
on main streets and back streets.
Metal building complexes
cover what was then a clover field,
a wheat field, a field of corn.
And in the distance, where the city
glowed into the sky at night, there is no night.
The glow surrounds this place now,
nudging the night sky further
toward some even more obscure distance.

There, where the funnel first stomped the ground,
twirling and twisting into itself,
there is cement. And now there are parking lots
and semi trucks where it came through
at an angle before turning into the city.

There, where the telephone lines stood
and were knocked to the ground,
a water tower balloons into the sky
in red and white swirls.
And where the fence leaned to the ground in the wind,
identical storage units
as uniform as the niches in a columbarium.

Look here for her.
Look in the cement and plowed-over lawn.
Pace out the distance from those trees
and there are only ghosts—
rebuilt remnants of lives
gone fumy and cloudy
by each decade.

And when I think to myself
of the sadness of this complete disappearance,
I am reminded that this too awaits all of us,
and even less than this.
Who, one day, will walk the paved over
remnants of my homestead,
following the heel-to-toe pattern of my house?
Who, in some impossible-to-imagine hazy future,
will look for the place I was
when I looked up and saw my darkest fear
staring me down from the sky above me?

Maria:

1. That day – June 20, 1957

We watched it
as it came rolling toward us.
Thilford and I knew
in our guts it was bad. Something that
big and that dark had to be bad.
And as it drew closer, it lunged at us
and we scampered.

Funnel west of the NDAC Memorial Union as it strikes Golden Ridge. (NDSU Institute for Regional Studies)

It squashed the house down on us
and, just when we thought
that was the worse,
the whole place exploded.
Splinters and boards
and the kitchen utensils.
It all rained upon us.

Afterward, Thilford stood up—
nothing more than a bump on his head.

But me—
I lay there, my arm as shattered
as the house.
My leg splintered
as the boards that lay over me.

2. September 9, 1961

Who would've thought he'd go first?
Who would've guessed he too would lose a leg
just like me,
just like some kind of weird sympathy pain.

But I wouldn't let them beat me.
I won't let those winds win.
No, they won't take me yet.
Not even after the surgeries, the metal plate,
my own amputation—
not even then will they get me.

He—
my Thilford—
he couldn't say the same
about the cancer that worked
its way through him,
first at the leg
(that went in '59)
and then
at the rest of him.

And now, alone, I face whatever that sky
will throw at me.
Let those winds blow.
Let them rage.
What more could they take at this point?
And when they do start gusting,
I will reach for that place
beside me, and I won't take my hand away
from that emptiness
until they've blown themselves out.

3. February 24, 1964

after a poem by Olav H. Hauge

The storm is gone now.
It is behind us
in some other place
on good days
we can barely remember.

Damage northwest of Fargo, where the tornado first struck. It was near here that Maria and Thilford Sanderson lived in 1957. (NDSU Institute for Regional Studies)

Not once
in all this time since
have we ever asked
why?
why was it I was there?
why there?
and why now? and not then?
Why was my leg
taken from me,
shattered to pieces
and embedded with grass, dirt,
and everything else
the wind gave me?
You were just there,
in the storm,
in the churning wind.

See, it is possible
to live every day.
It is possible to get up,
to go feed birds in the cold morning
and to watch
as they choose between
bread and snow.

The whole day is there to think about the wind
and there aren't enough hours in it
or in one's whole lifetime to consider it all.

And when it's done, you can sit down
and listen as a wind softer and more exotic
than the one you hear in your nightmares
comes to you, touching your face
and whispering to you in a language
as strange, yet beautiful
as Chinese
or Norwegian.

Grave of Maria Sanderson, Sunset Memorial Gardens, Fargo, North Dakota. (photo by author)

Theodore Udahl
(SuZ Templeton)

Theresa Udahl
(SuZ Templeton)

Mary Jean Udahl
(SuZ Templeton)

Mary Udahl (on left) with friend Janet Beyer in the Udahl home, Easter Sunday, April 21, 1957. Janet Beyer Syrup writes: "This photo was taken by Tinky Udahl in their living room. The cuckoo clock next to me was Tinky's pride and joy. It came from Germany, but don't remember how or why." (Janet Syrup)

Mary Udahl (on left) and Janet Beyer, Easter Sunday, April 21, 1957. Janet Syrup writes: "This photo was taken on the south side of the house with mailboxes on the east." (Janet Syrup)

Destroyed home of the Udahls (visible in the wreckage is the kitchen table and chairs) at 27th Avenue North. The body of Mary Jean was found in the wreckage of the home, and the bodies of Theodore and Theresa were found on the street outside the wreckage. Mary Jean had been adopted by the Udahls in 1955. (NDSU Institute for Regional Studies)

The visitation for the Udahl family, prior the funeral, Olivet Lutheran Church, Fargo, June 24, 1957. (NDSU Institute for Regional Studies)

Funeral for the Udahl family, Olivet Lutheran Church, Fargo, June 24, 1957.

(NDSU Institute for Regional Studies)

The caskets of the Udahls leaving Olivet Lutheran Church, 10th Street South in Fargo, June 24, 1957. (NDSU Institute for Regional Studies)

Graves of the Udahl family, North Prairie Lutheran Cemetery near Simcoe, North Dakota.
(photo by author)

North Prairie Lutheran Cemetery near Simcoe, North Dakota

Following funeral services on Monday, June 24, at Olivet Lutheran Church in Fargo, the bodies of Theodore and Theresa "Tinky" Udahl and their adopted daughter, Mary Jean, were sent to Velva, North Dakota, for additional services on the morning of Wednesday, June 26. That afternoon, they were buried near Simcoe, North Dakota.

1957 seems unreal
to me in this modern moment.
And here it is
chiseled out three times
in thick granite.

On this grassy rise
I stand firm against the wind,
in my coat, with my prying camera eye,
searching the grass
and chiseled granite for votives,
for the left-behind
proof someone
existed here.
Three people lived.
They were born and grew.
Three people were carried here
in polished silence
from the violence
and found in this ground peace.

Whatever debris
the wind summoned forth
in that distant year,
that strange arrangement
of numbers,
never made it this
far outstate.

Ghosts refuse
their trek back to
grass-covered rises in
rolling distant lands.
They exist only in those
unimaginable heights,
in star-filled places with names like
Delphinus
Ophiuchus
or Canes Venatici,
names which, for all I know
are made-up, exotic as distant planets.
Their ghosts exist
in the crushing weight
of shifting air and space.

Ghosts go into their silence in agony
and find in silence a refuge.
I find silence uncomfortable this day
that moves over me like a storm front.
It is an unpleasant end
to be crushed into silence
by experience and complacency.
That is an end reserved not for young people,
not for people like this family or myself,
but for old men
and trees.

The Munson Family c. 1957. Front row (l. to r.) Bradley, Darwin, Jeanette Irene. Back row: Gerald Munson holding Mary Beth, Mercedes Munson holding Lois Ann, Phyliss, and LeRoy (the only surviving child). (NDSU Institute for Regional Studies)

Gerald Munson (1912-1975), left, and Mercedes Munson (1921-2009), right, with their only surviving child, LeRoy, 14, after the tornado. (NDSU Institute for Regional Studies)

A brighter morrow

Gerald and Mercedes Munson:

1. 818 Twenty-fifth Street North

What would anyone expect of us, their parents—
two people who have grown apart
from each other by liquor and pain—
now faced with this reality?
Does anyone know how to mourn children?
Certainly they should be mourned—
tender as they are.
No one doubts that.
After all, they do what we wish
we could still do
and we resent it.
They sing
and shout
and tease.
They jostle each other
and live that single elusive moment
as though it will never end.

They spend their days
in an exuberance
that embarrasses us—
even us
who are never embarrassed—
simply because
we have lost our own joy.

Our joy—
or what tattered remnants we still cling to—
has been trampled into the earth.
We have shed our joy and have buried it
in a place we no longer remember.

We mourn our children
like this
because they are what we love
more even
than ourselves.

And so, when we read
their names in the newspaper,
when we hear them listed
one by one
on the television,
our voices crack and fail
with emotion.
We beg for sedatives—
any kind we can find.
We swallow them
quickly and desperately,
hoping for the numbing cloud
they produce to descend on us
and cover us completely.
When the cloud finally rises
we shrivel a bit
and, like them,
we die
in pieces.

Something in us tightens
when we listen, not really wanting to,
to their martyrologies.
We blink with disbelief
at what we are told
and can no longer remember with a clear mind.
We stare blankly even when we tell
the stories of how they stayed.

They stayed
for the surprise birthday party
they planned all day
for me—
their mother.
We sigh when we tell how Phyliss,
the oldest at sixteen,
on the phone
screamed, over the roar,
"it's going to hit, Mother!"
and then that silence
we will live with until we no longer live.

I—their mother—
hysterical with grief—
stood there, watching as they were found.
Each battered child,
all six of them, were picked
carefully from the shattered planks
and shingles, lifeless
as soaked pillows.

And our faces found
a mirror image in the face
of our neighbor Dick Shaw who carried
Jeanette Irene,
fragile and tender at five years old,
in his arms as he stumbled
toward me and the flashing camera bulb.
We looked with despair
into that newsprint
and knew
nothing in our lives would ever be
even remotely the same again.

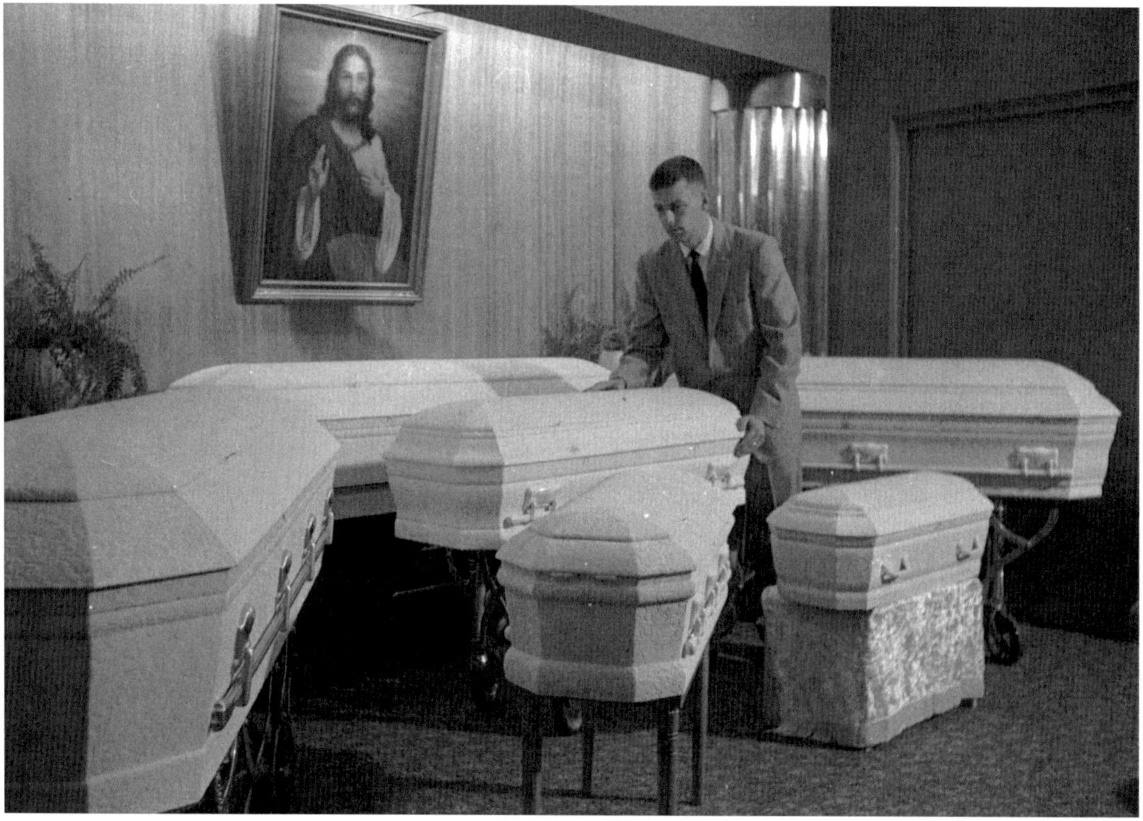

Edgar E. Wright Jr. (1934-2020) arranges the caskets of the Munson children at Wright Funeral Home, Moorhead, Minnesota, June 23, 1957. (NDSU Institute for Regional Studies)

The funeral for the Munson children at Trinity Lutheran Church, Moorhead, June 24, 1957.
(NDSU Institute for Regional Studies)

Hearses lined up on 7th Street South in front of Trinity Lutheran Church, Moorhead, following the Munson family funeral, June 24, 1957. (NDSU Institute for Regional Studies)

2. June 24, 1957. Trinity Lutheran Church, Moorhead, Minnesota.

Each white casket,
all six ranging in size
from adult to infant,
lay at angles before the altar.

Within them, what was left
lay tattered and torn,
broken at their most vital places.

No one could look long
at the display. No one could stare
except with a blank-eyed daze at each box.

Instead, we stared at the cross,
at the pulpit
at the floral displays
standing sentry over them
on spindly legs.

We looked at the floor
when the words of the pastor,
sacred and almost comforting,
rang out.

And when we sang,
we meant the words
that came to our lips,

Praise God, this hour of sorrow
Shall bring a brighter morrow;
I go to Paradise
My mother dear and father,
When round my grave you gather
Lay me to rest with songs of praise.

The hymn hummed
against the stony walls
and said what we could not.
That Monday afternoon,
it gave voice to
what little hope we could
muster at that hour.

The graveside service for the Munson children, Bethesda Cemetery (now Evergreen Memorial Cemetery), Moorhead, Minnesota. (NDSU Institute for Regional Studies)

Graves of the Munson family, Evergreen Memorial Cemetery, Moorhead, Minnesota. (photos by author)

MARY B.
1956 · 1957

LOIS A.
1954 · 1957

JEANETTE I.
1951 · 1957

BRADLEY L.
1948 · 1957

DARWIN J.
1945 · 1957

PHYLLIS L.
1940 · 1957

Betty and Don Titgen on their wedding day, November 15, 1951. (Lynn Brown)

November 15, 1951

Betty and Don's wedding day

The smell of cedar lingers,
giving up its scent
like the ghosts of these photos.

These ghosts

this woman in her stiff skirt,
a smear of magenta lipstick
framing her smile,

this man whose
dazzling youth
startles and humbles me

both stare back as though
the camera held up to them
revealed a future

more pleasant
than it would be.
Look how content they are.

They can't even imagine, in that halcyon moment,
the deaths that await them—
his, high in the black cloud

amid the debris,
hers, aching and lingering
in some etherized future neither could comprehend.

For now, in this November moment,
they smile. They cling to this
all-consuming blur of life

I, in my own dull moment,
can only
just barely fathom.

Grave of Donald Titgen, Holy Cross Cemetery, Fargo.
(photo by author)

Grave of Betty Titgen, Moorhead Memorial Gardens, Moorhead, Minnesota. (photo by author)

Betty&Don

"They have all gone into the world of light!"
—Henry Vaughan

My grandmother, Phoebe Olson:

1.

When our dead
die like that
we,
uncomfortable as we are to do it,
tend to canonize.
We make saints of our own.

We learn to forget
scandals and failings.
We convince ourselves
that to speak ill of our dead
is a sin.

Even in the cemetery,
we never walk on their graves.
We step lightly
hopping and skipping about
not because we're superstitious.
We do it because it's disrespectful.

And when we do say their names,
we whisper them,
just as we do the Sacred Names
we use in our prayers.

We whisper their names
because, for us, they are sacred—
they are precious and holy
in ways they would find uncomfortable.

2.

For years afterward,
that was how we said their names.

Betty&Don.

One word,
one incident
in some family past,
like the great-uncle who died
homeless and alcoholic
buried in the Pauper's Cemetery
or the crazy cousin
sent to the loony bin
in Jamestown, where she died
of Parkinson's.
They were names only
and a violent end. Eventually,
no one would even
call it unfair anymore.
They simply talked about it,
always in June,
and even then as though
it was a disgrace.

Betty&Don.
Just that one word,
that one event
in some strange 1950s past
I could barely even imagine.
And, for me, not even that.
Only later would they
become more real,
a grainy yellowing newspaper photo
from their wedding,

their death certificates which revealed
only the gruesome details,
the story of a first child
who died at birth.

Even later they became
a pair of gravestones
his in the Catholic Cemetery
a slab of military gray
set into the encroaching sod
with its inscription

DONALD ELROY TITGEN
NORTH DAKOTA
CPL 9213 TECH-SVC UNIT
OCT 12 1930 JUNE 20 1957

The stone was almost lost to the grass
until one hot day
I sawed away the thick earth
and edged the stone,
revealing its inscription
for the cemetery workers
who would place a flag there
each Memorial Day.

And hers,
a name and dates
between two engraved roses

MRS. BETTY LOU TITGEN
1936 - 1960

molded from a bronze plate
turning green as cemetery grass,
on the south side of Moorhead.

Betty&Don.
That one word.
And yet, it was ultimately
all about separation.
Two deaths in two different years,
as it is normally
when old people die.
Not people in their twenties.
And even then, two graves
in two separate cemeteries,
kept apart by something
vaguely religious—
she, Protestant,
he, Catholic—
though no
one would admit it.

If it would happen now, the rules
would be relaxed, we say.
Then, it was different. Then...
we didn't know what to do.
Who was there to tell us?
Who'd ever been through *this*?
Who'd ever lost their families
like *this*?

And we, in the long clear days
in the middle of June, find ourselves
wondering: what if?
What if the storm went north.
Or south.
What if this had never happened?
What if Betty&Don had just stayed put,
instead rushing home
from wherever they were
to get to the kids?
What if?

They would be facing now
what they looked upon that day,
only now they'd be better prepared.
They'd have gone to their final days
as we all should,
aching and complaining,
mourned by children and grandchildren
who would feel guilt for not visiting as often,
who would seethe secretly for parental faults
who would move on to face their own ends
in due course.

In those long June afternoons
we ask the same questions,
we shake our heads,
we make the trek from
one cemetery to the other,
laying our silk flowers there.
Then we turn away for our cars,
glancing up at the skies which
spew storms quickly on these hot days
and stiffen a bit
when we hear thunder.

A street sign at the intersection of 13th Avenue and 8th Street North bent over with a piece of sheet metal wrapped around it. Also visible is a fire hydrant in the foreground and a ruined home in the background. (NDSU Institute for Regional Studies)

O Salutaris

O Salutaris Hostia
Quae caeli pandis ostium.
—St. Thomas Aquinas

Don:

What did we ask for in our lives?
After weeks of work and toil and loss,
all we needed was a break.

So what if we were at the Brass Rail
on Front Street?
Does anyone care?
And does it matter?

Or what if we were
at the movies with another couple?
Gunfight at the O.K. Corral
had just opened that day
and promised us a glimpse of a glory
we rarely saw
as it rose before us on the screen
in all its VistaVision splendor
at the Fargo Theatre.

Does anyone know the panic,
the fear we carried with us
when the sirens blared
and we tore off for home—
to the kids?

We prayed—
we did!—
for the kids.

In that moment we prayed
that my sister Molly
would take them away
and find safety—
somewhere in the opposite direction
of the storm,
somewhere something in us
told us to go to as well.

What did we ask for?
Did we ask to be delivered,
even as I had Betty get down on the floor
as I dragged the mattress over
and laid it on her?
Did I ask for anything in that moment
my friend and I prostrated ourselves
on top of the mattress and held on to what we could,
the roar of the storm so loud in our ears,
the rumble of it beneath us
and above us
and around us?

What did I ask for
when I found myself freed
from that anchoring beneath me
and was lifted up
into the swirling darkness above me?

I couldn't ask.
Instead, I accepted what the answer was
and let it
like the cyclone forces that raged around me
do what it had to do to me
and to us
and to all that we knew and held dear.

Her Prayer

after Kadya Molodowsky

Betty:

Don't let me fall!
Let me not fall through the long night
as a stone falls to the hard ground.

Don't let my hands chaff and blister
in the high dry winds
and peel like bark from trees.

Don't let me fall
as the wind beats leaves from
the trees and scatters them across the grass.

When the angry storm rises
and kicks up dirt from the earth,
screaming at me in the long dusk,

don't let me be like a fly
shivering and grasping at the glass pane
as autumn dies.

Don't let me fall!
Throughout my short life
I have asked for so much.

Let me rather be like
a seed that falls from a grass blade
in the park near the house I grew up in.

Like that seed let me flourish
and then let me die
quietly and unnoticed in some future dusk.

And in that moment
sow in me your breath
as seeds are sown in the warm, fresh-tilled earth.

Finding Him

1.

The Priest/Poet:

Young men die every day.
Wars kill them by scores.
They meet their ends
by guns and cars and all sorts of violence.
A few die quietly in their beds—
as though it was
the most natural thing to do.

Few go flying,
limbs flailing,
into the cyclonic winds
made black by dirt and debris.

Few go up,
caught up in that turbine of forces,
clutching at air
only to find
air.

Wreckage in north Fargo the evening of the tornado. (NDSU Institute for Regional Studies)

2.

A housewife from Golden Ridge:

When I emerged
from my basement
I found my house gone—
a few boards and a scattering of shingles
and that was it—
and one of my neighbors

Don Titgen

lying on the boulevard—
his hair
white as a summer cloud.
Can you imagine that!
That handsome
dark-haired man!
Can you imagine what
it must've been like
up there
in those dark winds—
what it must've been like
to make your hair
turn *white* like that?

There he was,
blocks from their home,
a 2x4 in his chest.
Or was it in both of his legs?

I don't remember anymore.
Or maybe
I just don't want to.

3.

The Priest/Poet:

Later, I listened
to the gruesome details
much as one would listen
to war stories
or news of plane crashes.

And, at that age,
you could imagine it,
the 2x4,
the violence of it all.

And most of all—
his hair.

4.

My mother's cousins:

It was white—
his hair.
White
like a cloud
is white.

We can't even imagine it.

Jesus!
White!

And it's then we pause,
we shake our heads,
seeing it all there in their minds.
And it's then
we ask ourselves,

"What could it be—
what horrible thing—
makes
a twenty-seven year old's
hair turn
white?
What happened
up there
in that dark place
above us all?"

5.

The undertaker:

There wasn't much I could do.
The dirt was imbedded deep into his skin.
And even makeup can't cover that.

And his hair.
There was no need to dye it back
to the color I imagined it was
from the photo I was given.
It's easier just to lay a swath of purple silk
over his face,
over his folded hands,
speckled with deep-buried grit and debris.
Even then though
you can see the hair.
Even then,
through the cloth,
you can see that
bleached-out color.

And when I was done, we held off
the burial for days, waiting.
Would she join him?
Would I have to reconstruct
what the winds did
to her face?
Would we set her hair
and reconstruct her into the beauty she was
smiling back from that same wedding photo?

And then what?
A double funeral?
A Protestant laid next to him
in the Cathedral? A Catholic

left in the hearse while
the Lutheran pastor read
scriptures
and a prayer that ended
"Mercifully grant that after this life,
we, with all Thy saints,
may be received into everlasting joy..."

And then what?
There are rules.
People don't understand
how things are.

Catholics don't just go off to secular places—
cemeteries where the bronze markers
all lie flat and uniform
flush to the flat, featureless prairie—
a vast forgettery of graves
where her family would want her.
And certainly the powers-that-be
wouldn't let her be set down
in that place where they buried nuns
and their bishops.

She survived though,
if that's what you want to call it,
and he went off to the place he belonged.
At the wake,
there in the hushed chapel
his casket lay open.
They came forward,
every one of them,
and I heard them gasp
as they looked upon
his silk-shrouded body—

that pale shock of hair
visible underneath,
a rosary carefully entwined in his stiff fingers.
And on the crucifix, the corpus,
tinted the color of a raisin,
stared downward into that tragedy
from the satin-lined inner coffin lid
because that's what it always did.

In the Cathedral
the Monsignor stood at the High Altar
and sang the words
Ipsis, Domine, et omnibus in Christo
quiescentibus, locum refrigerii, lucis et pacis,
ut indulgeas, deprecamur.
Per eumdem Christum Dominum nostruim. Amen.
then sprinkled water
and incense over the palled coffin
while I watched the in-laws frown,
holding clean stiff hankies
to their sunburned noses.

Aerial view looking north toward the airport. (NDSU Institute for Regional Studies)

6.

My aunt Shirley:

It was a long, slow ride north
to Holy Cross Cemetery,
to that place few of us,
stiff-lipped and good Protestants that we were,
dared to venture, repelled as we were
by the statues and the difficult invocations of saints
engraved in stone
we squinted at
and never could understand.

We talked later of it—
of the unfairness of it all,
and how everything
we thought we knew
had been tossed about
and had been thrown—
shattered and lifeless—
at our feet.

(From left to right) **Shirley Olson** (the author's aunt)**, Betty Lou Olson and Joyce Olson** (the author's mother)**. Fargo. March 29, 1943.**

(Joyce Parsley)

7.

My mother:

Finally—
in the end—
we just shrugged our shoulders
as we do
and let it go.

To think of it too much
hurt.
It caused an ache
to grow in us
we struggled against for years
until eventually—
finally,
thank God—
even it numbed away.

She lived

Betty Lou suffered severe brain injuries as well as losing an eye. Never regaining consciousness, she was hospitalized at St. Luke's Hospital in Fargo and other Fargo nursing homes, before she was moved to a rehabilitation center in Wahpeton, North Dakota, six months before her death on January 16, 1960. Her father had died three weeks earlier on December 25, 1959.

She lived. Someone might
even have said it was a miracle
until they saw her,
one eye knocked out,
the wound on her head,
the coma that took hold
and never gave up
except to pneumonia
two and a half years later.

She lived. Even when they
played records—
none of them remember which ones—
for her in the nursing home,
even when they told her
of her girls, who continued to grow
without her.
They were certain she heard them.

"She responded to the music," they said.
"We saw her ourselves, the eyelids
almost keeping time. A slight
movement of her pinkie."

And whenever anyone would enter the room
she opened her eyes, as though she knew—
as though she were waiting
for someone.

Meanwhile,
miracles of this sort
were more difficult
than death.

With miracles, one offers thanks.
With death, one mourns.
But with this, one…
suffers. One waits and prays,
careful in what one says
knowing the answers aren't
what we want or expect.

Miracles like this
are simply taken for what they are.
They are clutched after
as they dodge
and escape.
A moment is taken
to cherish this moment or the next,
uncertain of the one that follows it.
One rages silently,
because that is what is done.
When crying,
one does it alone,
in the car
or late at night.
At church
prayers turn quickly
into cold stones.

The tender insides of one's mouth
are bitten
until they bleed.
And, on good days,
there are forced smiles
and comments such as
"God is good"
and on even better days,
one can even believe it.

The wind, one dusk

Laura Schoenherr (1888-1957) lived at 821 26th Street North. Critically injured in the storm, she died one month later on July 16, 1957.

Laura Schoenherr
(SuZ Templeton)

after a poem by
Antonio Machado

Laura:

The wind, one dusk
called me.
It said my name
and when it did
I turned
and saw it.

The wind in the evening
sang my name
with a tune
lower than ones
the organ in church
played.

The wind said
Laura
and when it did,
I smelled jasmine.

The wind, one evening
said to me,
"Laura,
exchange with me
if you would
this smell of jasmine
for the odors of your roses."

I said to the wind,
"roses? I haven't grown
roses in years.
My roses died one fall
years back and never reappeared.
The garden I grew them in
is now full of dead flowers."

The wind persisted,
growling low and dark
at my window
out here on the outskirts of town.
It said,
"Fine then. Give me
the dried petals.
Give me the leaves
made yellow by death.
And give me too
the water from the pump
you used
to nourish them."

I did.
And the wind took them then and went
on through the city.
In the end, it left me here, dying.
For less than a month
I suffered
before I finally gave up
and let myself go.
And I laid there
waiting as the smell
of jasmine faded
in the rain.

On that last day
I said to myself
with a voice
only I could hear
and even then
couldn't recognize,
"What did you do, Laura?
What did you do?
What did you do
to the garden
entrusted to you?"

Grave of Laura Schoenherr (with last named misspelled), Zion Cemetery, Chaffee, North Dakota. (photo by author)

View looking north on the 700 block of 27th Street North, showing a house and a row of mailboxes. In the background is the Golden Ridge Lutheran Church. Both house and church were completely destroyed by the tornado of June 20, 1957. (NDSU Institute for Regional Studies)

Stained glass window in the rebuilt Golden Ridge Lutheran Church, Fargo.
(photo by author)

Golden Ridge Lutheran Church

Golden Ridge Lutheran Church was organized in the early 1950s to serve the Golden Ridge/College Addition 1 neighborhood by Pastor Alvin Keller (the pastor who married my mother and her first husband in 1954). Charter members of the church included Theodore, Theresa, and Mary Jean Udahl, who lived across the street from the church. The first service held in the newly completed building was held on June 3, 1956. It was dedicated on October 28, 1956. The tornado destroyed the church and the homes of thirty-two members.

"No longer the Lamb
but the idea of it."
—R.S. Thomas

The Blood
spilled
lies there.

The corporal sops it.
And on the paten,
the Body

like their bodies
lies broken,
more perfectly

than the broken bodies
that were set into
the earth

and covered
with sod.
And when everyone looks

at It, held up to them
to adore,
they adore It.

And they remember.
They say to
that broken Body,

break us, O Body,
not as we wish
but as You wish us

to be broken. And
when You wish,
put us back again.

American Lutheran Church on 12th Avenue North in Fargo. The church lost its roof in the tornado. Debris litters the lawn in front of the building and the cross at the top of the steeple is bent over. The author's mother was married for the first time in this church in 1954.

(NDSU Institute for Regional Studies)

Miracles

What does anyone know
of miracles?
They—my mother's family—
certainly stopped expecting them early on

sometime around
the time they went to church and were confirmed.
They packed them away
with the cards they received,

with the certificate the pastor signed.
And, later, when they needed answers to prayers
they forgot how to ask for them
little more than recognize them

when they came falling
into their lives
like sunlight.
Others were better

at recognizing them.
The Sisters of the Presentation
in the days after the tornado
saw miracles everywhere amid the wreckage

of the convent.
Not a single statue of Our Lady
was destroyed. Not one statue
of St. Joseph

was overturned.
But Lutherans—like my relations—lamented.
The cross on the church
in which my mother married the first time

was wrestled free and thrown
to the ground
much as they did
when angry with God, if they dared.

The Lutheran Church
in Golden Ridge, the one
the Udahls lived across
the street from—

the one in which "Tinky" Udahl
dusted the pews
early every Sunday morning
before services

was leveled,
knocked flat as
the mythical walls of
Canaanite cities

falling at the trumpet call.
Around it lay shriveled hymnals
and pages of scripture
no longer sacred,

misused and made sacrilege
by the heavy rain that fell
later that night.
On each page, the word

"God"
lay smudged with mud,
trampled upon
and empty of meaning.

And one perfect image;
a painting,
a head-and-shoulders
portrait of the Savior

staring off in the direction
the storm came,
lay unscathed while
everything around it

collapsed into rumble.
Everyone else
who made it
somehow struggled through.

What was divine about it?
my family wondered
and still do.
What holiness

hid itself
like Job's
God
within the wind?

Mother St. Kevin Brennan (1904-1989) and Sisters Antonine Foy (1922-2016) and and Scholastica Marquart (1901-1999) of the Sisters of the Presentation of the Blessed Virgin Mary survey damage done to Sacred Heart Convent, North Broadway in Fargo. (NDSU Institute for Regional Studies)

Mother St. Kevin Brennan and Sisters Genevieve Murphy (1895-1978) and Antonine Foy stand beside a pine tree that was blown through a window at Sacred Heart Convent, Fargo.
(NDSU Institute for Regional Studies)

Rain falls on a wrecked building near Fargo on the evening of the tornado.

(NDSU Institute for Regional Studies)

The so-called "rope cloud" over El Zagal Bowl and Clubhouse in north Fargo, as the storm dissipates over the Red River. (NDSU Institute for Regional Studies)

II.

After the Storm

"The sky is relentlessly sapphire,
and the past is happening quickly."
—Agha Shahid Ali

After the storm

"Shine, o shine,
unfalsifying sun, on this sick scene."
—Marianne Moore

My mother's cousin, Judith:

1.

After the storm
all night
we heard what sounded like a train.
Not a freight train, the one we heard
when the cloud hit the ground
and plowed its way toward Minnesota.
No, this train just hummed all night,
as though it were spinning its wheels in place.
And every few minutes
flames shot into the sky
from the north side of town,
where everything was leveled.
Tall blue flames with glaring white
in their centers, like the atomic bomb flashes
we saw in the newsreels.
Just flames,
all night
rising into the rain-filled sky,
fizzling eventually into quickly
dying stars.

It was the transformers
someone said,
blown apart by the winds.
It was electricity
bypassed into
broken lines and exposed
to dense night air.

When the kids awoke
during the night to the sound
and saw the flashes in the sky,
they believed it was
flying saucers
flashing overhead.
While some were excited by the prospect,
others cried and whimpered
all night as the north side of town died.

Everyone else knew better.
They, who in the long dark night
with no electricity, listened patiently to the rain
to the explosions
and to the steady hum of a train
going nowhere.

Looking south on Broadway showing three automobiles on the street with one flipped on its roof. In the background is the Sacred Heart Convent. (NDSU Institute for Regional Studies)

2.

After the storm,
after the rains that came
and drenched every
exposed thing,
that next morning,
the day dawned
cool and airy.

In that dawn,
we picked through the boards
and broken glass.
We looked in every overturned car
and under every fallen roof.

What we were searching for
could never be found however
there in that shattered world.

What we sought
hid from us.
It eluded us
as we chased it down,
through dusty alleys
filled with rubble,
through blasted open buildings.

The last time we saw it—
that ephemeral thing,
in those unending days
before the air turned cool
and the bite of autumn
touched our burning faces—
it was above us, smiling
and waving and turning
this way and that
as it made its way
to wherever it was going.

Crushed automobile parked with other damaged cars at the Red River Valley Fairgrounds in north Fargo (where Fargo North High School now stands). (NDSU Institute for Regional Studies)

Solstice

My grandmother, Phoebe:

1.

I later remembered
that it was the solstice
that day.
I, like everyone, delighted
in that summer heat that came upon us
so suddenly
after months of death-like cold.

We rejoiced in it.
And as we did,
I wondered
how could it do to them
anything even
remotely
harmful?

Mike O'Leary uses a telephone set up temporarily on a pole at 13th Street and 13th Avenue North. The phone booth on that corner had been blown a block away.

(NDSU Institute for Regional Studies)

2.

That summer season
worked away inside us
for months. From
blizzards
to the thaw
to the overflowing gullies
it came too
like a poem we longed to write
but couldn't.
Poems are frivolous things,
a waste of time and energy.
Still, in our way,
we recognized the verse of the season
with its unending stanzas,
with its dotted miniscule i's
and its lower-case persistent c's
and its sense of potential joy.

Like that day
it floated above us,
taunting us to take up
the pen, to open the book
and put the words down.
It teased us to sing.
As if we could—
or would—
sing!

3.

The deluge of rain the night before
turned
cool and airy,
a mist really
as it wet our faces.
Out driving, my husband, Ted, and I stopped
alongside the curve of highway
north of town,
to survey the destruction of the tornado,
There in the ditch were cattle,
shattered and twisted
as wind-blown quilts
scattered about. Tangled
metal and splintered wood
lay in the field. A dead fox
eyed us with gray-filmed eyes
from the rain-soaked ditch.
Staring back, we shivered
against the warm gray sky,
overcast with clouds thick
as the bloated stomachs
of those cows.

4.

We have lugged the poem
of that unending day with us, wherever
we went, where the words
trembled into sore heaps upon them.
Vowels and commas and periods
fell as rain did,
thudding and clunking
into our day
like the hail
after a funnel-laden
storm.

A piano lies among debris near the southeast corner of 12th Avenue and University Drive North.
(NDSU Institute for Regional Studies)

5.

The day went on
and on and we
went with it.
The poem of that day swayed
on the pages of every book
we found, rain-swollen and warped,
tossed into our backyard.
It lolled this way
and that way,
faking the motions
of the twisting darkness
the night before as it wound its way
through that almost isolated place.
We could almost see it still,
dancing as the rain
danced,
as the poem
danced and twirled around us.
We could almost see it
from wherever we stood—
shaking our heads at it
in disbelief.

Dick Shaw carrying the body of Jeanette Irene Munson from the wreckage of the Munson home, June 20, 1957.
(Cal Olson, the Forum)

These hands

The icon of the disaster quickly became the photo taken by Fargo Forum *photographer Cal Olson (1924-2009) of 21-year-old Dick Shaw carrying the body of 5-year-old Jeanette Irene Munson.*

1. July, 1952

in memory:

Mary Shaw
(January 17, 1917 – July 19, 1952)

Lillian Shaw
(March 9, 1946 – July 19, 1952)

John Shaw
(July 12, 1944 – July 23, 1952)

It wasn't wind, but fire that started
the world coming undone. Fire raged
and the world turned dark and silent.
Fire, despite what romantic people think,
doesn't purify. It destroys.
It blackens and covers with
soot and smoke what it leaves behind.

Most families die slowly, as they should.
For most of us, it happens, one by one.
Our grandparents give way to their aging children.
Sometimes, though,
families die like this,
taken as quickly as the wind
in those elements.

A mother and daughter
found charred beside
a burned-out bedframe.
And five days later, eight-year-old John,
who escaped through a window
and shouted, "Mommy's in there!
I could hear her screaming!"
died, burned and bruised
and gasping for his mother.

No one,
especially Dick,
asked later, where the wind was that morning
to exhaust the fire and stop it. No one
raged in anger or shook their fists
at skies filled, in mid-July,
with clouds simple as pillows.

No one asked anything,
even as all three were placed in one coffin
and buried one hot July afternoon
on a pine-covered rise
overlooking a lake. They simply turned inward,
pursing their pale faces with silence
one summer after another
until those same clouds boiled and turned
black as char in the west.

Grave of Mary, Lillian, and John Shaw, Oak Grove Cemetery, Detroit Lakes, Minnesota. (photo by author)

2. June 20, 1957

Who knew what happened just before
the camera's flash?
Who bothered to ask? He,
in those moments before, helped his
pregnant sister and her husband
out of their car and into a ditch.
He then hugged a tree
as the funnel hit. His legs flew
straight out from him,
like the exaggerated posturing
one sees in a Buñuel film
but which in reality seems absurd.

Dazed and shaken, he wandered the neighborhood
and came upon the pile of lumber
that only moments before was the Munson home.
Braving nails and debris, he found two of them
and carried them, tender as babies, to the street.
If he noticed the camera's flash
it didn't show on his face.
He didn't think twice about it until the next day
when it appeared on front page of the *Forum*,
slightly out-of-focus and not even
remotely as gruesome as it actually was.
But he never said a thing.
He only tucked it away and lived with it
as we all live with our secret pains.

Who bothered to ask, after all? And what
would shy boys say of such things anyway?
What could they say when they're left
even more quiet by the events of
a world coming undone around them
moment by moment,
summer by summer?
What would boys like that say,
even if their photos,
snapped in moments so candid
they should never be shared,
stare back from every newspaper in the country
and win Pulitzer Prizes for people you don't even know?

3. 52 Main Avenue

in memory:

Fred Shaw
(February 4, 1896 – February 14, 1963)

John "Cyclone" Johnson
(September 23, 1881 – February 14, 1963)

There was a bleakness to that forgotten place,
to those ramshackle houses
under the Main Avenue bridge
there along the river
between Fargo and Moorhead.
It's all gone now,
razed to the ground by
Urban Redevelopment,
plowed so completely into the grass
we can't even imagine it
now in this pristine place
of bikepaths and landscaping.

It was worse then in winter,
in those tarpaper shacks
in bleak February when the air
promises a spring it cannot deliver.

What do you say when they find your father
like that, beaten beyond recognition,
killed by a knife, a hammer, a coal shovel,
a hatchet? Two elderly
men, snuffed out in a shack
on a frozen afternoon
out here
in eastern North Dakota?

What do you do when
the Mayor of Fargo,
Herschel Lashkowitz himself,
says on seeing the bodies,
that it was the "most
savage, fiendish crime
I have ever seen"?

What do you do after that? You do what
you did before,
what you know best. You bury them.
You turn from their graves,
wiping the hands you used to hold dead children,
and you disappear into the only possession you have—
your silence.

4. Montana, August 29, 1969

The poet Richard Hugo
would write, around this time,
of Montana, *You are lost*
in miles of land without people, without
one fear of being found, in the dash
of rabbits, soar of antelope, swirl
merge and clatter of streams.

And he was right. This land is easy
to lose yourself within. And the wind,
that Montana wind,
could blow straight through to Fargo
if it could. It would go
right over hundreds of miles of
rolling ranchland and fields,
over serpentine rivers
and sparse scatterings of trees.

This wind, in late August, is different
than the winds of June. They promise
something gentler,
something cooler and more pleasant
than the raging violence of early summer.

The wind in August knows.
It has seen it all before.
It understands that
we all die. And when we do,
hopefully we will go into it quietly.
Why remark about that last
involuntary sound we make,
that last gasp we fight to control and can't?
Why chatter on about it? Who would
listen anyway? Only the wind.

So when he goes, he goes
silently, in a car,
gasping for breath
just as he did once before,
in a windstorm
in some distant time and place.
He goes and lets people wonder
what happened to him. Was it his own
hand that did it? Was it foul play?
Or did it just happen?
An accident, like fires
or weather supercells that mutate into
violent turbines?

Everyone dies
but everyone doesn't
leave behind an image
of themselves,
a fading last moment, frozen
in mid-motion, their faces
captured in profile, their hair
hanging in disarray, their legs
ready to give out beneath them.

Not everyone goes into that final silence
remembered for acts of kindnesses
done for five year old girls
who will never be able to reach out to them
to touch their shocked face
and say to them as night falls,
Thank you.

Grave of Dick Shaw, Oak Grove Cemetery, Detroit Lakes, Minnesota. (photo by author)

A flagpole at 1310 Broadway bent by the tornado. (NDSU Institute for Regional Studies)

The Wind Will Take It

after a poem by Marguerite de Navarre

The survivors:

If everything you worked for
and longed for,
if everything you loved
and hoped in,
is taken from you
one summer evening
    shrug your shoulders
    and say, "so be it."
    There is no grand art
    in mourning
    or loss.
    No one is going to feel
    any more sorry for you
    than this.
    And what's the use of pity after all?
    Because, as we know,
the wind will take it.

If anyone praises you
for your bravery in the face of death.
If anyone marvels
at your strength
as you make it through the funerals
without breaking down or crying
    ignore them.
    This kind of praise never sustains.

It will not comfort you
in those long nights
with no one else around
to stroke your aching shoulders
or caress your face
numb with crying.
Besides, who knows better than you that
the wind will take it.

If anyone says to you
in your grief
you're a saint.
If they praise you
for clutching at your faith
even when it seems
heaven has turned against you
turn away from them politely
and let their compliments
return to them unclaimed.
Sainthood, like all praise,
is fluff these days.
And, like fluff,
the wind will take it.

And if your luck changes
and you find yourself surrounded
by everything you ever wanted in this life,
by money, houses, cars,
and that evasive thing, love,
by all the things that bring
to your mouth a taste like sweet cane sugar,
say "thank you," but in doing so
remember how quickly it can all go again.
Say, "yes, it's nice" but maybe soon
the wind will take it.

If they tell you
those who died here
never were.
If they say,
their graves are empty,
their names are random letters
on eroding slabs of stone or bronze,
and we have forgotten,
once and for all,
the sound of their voices.
If they say
there was no storm,
no destruction.
If they say
"look around! it never happened!—
it was only a dream,
a nightmare one long summer night,
        they are lying to you.
        Stand up to them and say
        "You're wrong!"
        for, as we all know,
        now better than before
the wind will take it.

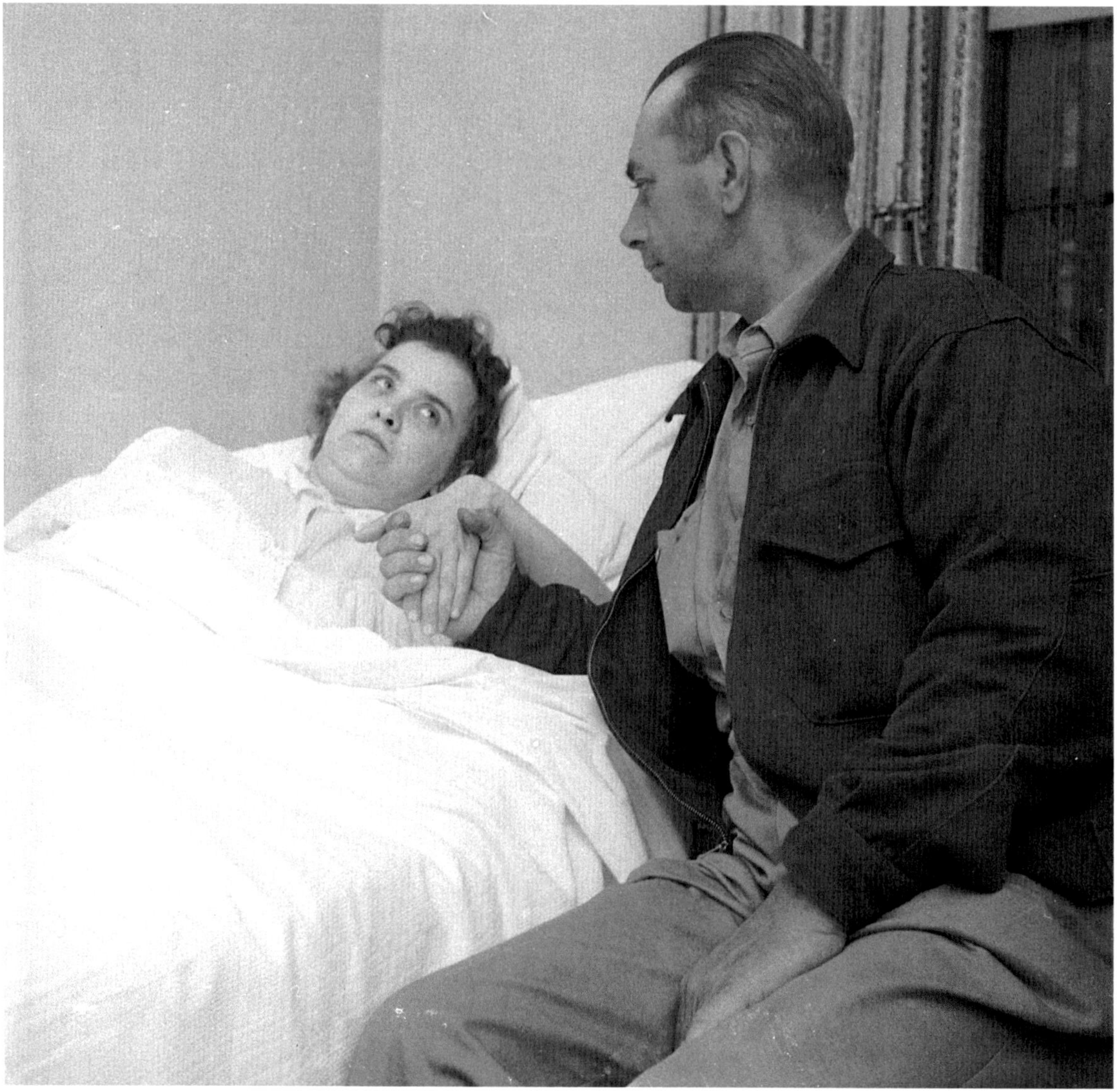

Mercedes Munson, with her husband, Gerald, in St. John's Hospital on June 21, 1957. She was hospitalized after a physical and emotional collapse. The Munsons divorced the following month. (NDSU Institute for Regional Studies)

Mercedes

Mercedes Munson Erickson was the mother of the six Munson children who died in the tornado. June 20, 1957, was also her thirty-sixth birthday. In the years following the tragedy, despite a divorce from Gerald Munson in July 1957 and her own personal demons, she emerged as a symbol of and voice for the victims and survivors of the storm. She died on September 4, 2009.

1. June 20, 2007

I lean down into the grass—
this grass which
one day soon

will hold my ashes.
I lean down and
I know they are right there—

just out of my reach,
each one laid out
side-by-side

head-to-feet.
I lean down into the grass
and whisper to them.

They don't hear me—
me, their mother
who sings

as I sang to them
once long ago
in the night.

In their sleep
they don't hear me, or anything.
In their sleep they are unaware

of me
their mother
crying for them still.

They are unaware
of everything
even the roots

growing slowly
down to them
through the rich, dark earth.

2.

Do I dare ask
for mercy?

At this stage,
overwhelmed by all

that has been done,
can I? It's done.

I know it
and I can't change

a thing. Even if I could
would I?

except
maybe

for one more chance
one more moment

in which we could sit down
together once again

and share something
with each other—

something as beautiful
and joyful

as a birthday party
with cake and decorations

and we could share
with one another

something that would make us
laugh.

3. September 4, 2009

after a poem by Miguel Hernandez

Today I am ready for suffering.
I am ready to have no friends.
I am ready to reach deep within myself
and tear out my heart,
pulling it from me by the root
like a tooth.
I am ready to bury its ashes here
in a small grave surrounded by
the graves of my children.

Today I am ready for the thorn
that grows hard and stiffens within me.
Today I am ready to cry tears that unclenched themselves
from me and hang from my face
heavy as metal.

Today I am ready for my destiny.
I am ready for death to come
to me like a surprise party
on my birthday.
I am ready for the swords—
all six of them to pierce the ashes of my heart.
I am ready for the wind
that cuts me at my core
like a dull axe.
I am ready for it to take me up
higher than any church steeple
and throw me down to the earth.

Today I am ready for this poem—
for these words I have carried hidden inside me
for over fifty unbearable summers.
I am ready
for these words written with ink from
the pitch-colored inkwell of my heart,
for the curves and dashes of the letters of my children's names,
for the goodbyes and the stay-puts
of that one final phone call, interrupted.

I am ready for that star—
that poisoned star—
under which I was born only to appear again
as it does every year at this solstice time.
I am ready for my grief to end,
this grief that has weighed on me more than
the scattered joys I can now only vaguely remember.

I am ready for love.
My love for my children has left me paralyzed,
my arms useless.
My eyes only see through the stinging blur of tears.
My mouth slurs the words I have only now found
to say.

I am ready to show everyone what lies within me.
Do you see what it is?
It is this mourning.
If I could
I would cut it from me.
But with what? What knife,
what scissors cut that deep?

I am ready for a day like yesterday.
Tomorrow will be no different.
But today…
today I am ready.
Today I am desperate from suffering,
my heart shattered like a fishbowl
my words written with the blood of dying sparrows.

Today,
I am nothing but heart.

Today I am ready.
I am ready to let my heart go.
Who ever had a bigger heart than me?
And with it, who knew more bitterness?

Today, I am ready
and I don't know why.
I only know how and where I am going.
Today, like every day,
I am ready—
if need be—
for life to keep going on.

Grave of Mercedes Munson Erickson, Evergreen Memorial Cemetery, Moorhead, Minnesota. (photo by author)

Ghostly

> "…in knowing of God and of ghostly things…"
> —Walter Hilton

Ghosts always obsessed me,
not vampires or ghouls or werewolves.
Ghosts, unlike other fictions,
seemed more plausible. Ephemeral shapes
and faces, like all our dead,
seemed possible
and in those long dark nights
I could almost hear them,
wandering about, sighing sadly
in the hallway or shuffling around the corner.

Ghosts *could* be real I thought.
Death, after all, was a reality for me,
and because it was,
I hoped, in my way, that it was more
than just a mysterious all-encompassing darkness
we braced ourselves against
when we paused long enough
to consider it.

I hoped
even before religious belief piqued
that somehow we went some *where,*
that we went on in some *way*—
it didn't matter how,
just as long as we didn't stop being,
curled up into a nihilism
that seemed more tragic
than anything else I could imagine.

I believed that they—
the ones who had gone into that strange, murky place,
that foggy other-world—
knew us and saw us,
observing our fumbling attempts at life and living.

I became obsessed with *them*—
all of them, who were laid out by the winds
on that steamy June afternoon twelve years before I was born.
Their mystery stuck in me
the way romantic crushes did.
Like those attempts at love,
I would lie awake at night,
sick in my guts with longing.

Their ghosts
hovered over me—
pale and blue—
as I imagined them
in the perpetual poses of their wedding photos
and birthday party snapshots
and postured portraits—
sepia-colored—
with padded shoulders and double-breasted suits,
in full A-Line skirts and crinoline—
lifted up into those winds
we came to despise
like the perfectly depicted martyrdom of saints
portrayed in icons or retablos.

It was the mystery of them
that grew within me
year after year.
It dominated my thinking
the way God
or love
or poetry
would obsess me at other times in my life.

Those ghosts hung there above me
hovering about in some distant heaven.
The oppressive air of
their presence was made more real
as I struggled one long summer to read Walter Hilton
and his eerily descriptive phrases.
I would repeat them like incantations.
"Ghostly affection," I would say.
"ghostly mirth," and
"ghostly sight," and thought I knew
what they meant.

After all,
this was my ghostly mirth.
This was my ghostly sight—
staring into the murky unknown
and seeing what others didn't.
And what I felt for them
then and always
was truly ghostly affection.

Ghosts have always obsessed me.
Even now, praying for them,
reciting for them the requiem masses most never had,
absolving what they did or failed to do,
I bond to them in that ghostly way
that I bond with anyone I bury.
And, like ghosts, we grasp at each other
across the abyss,
our voices sounding to the other
like the first rumble of approaching thunder.

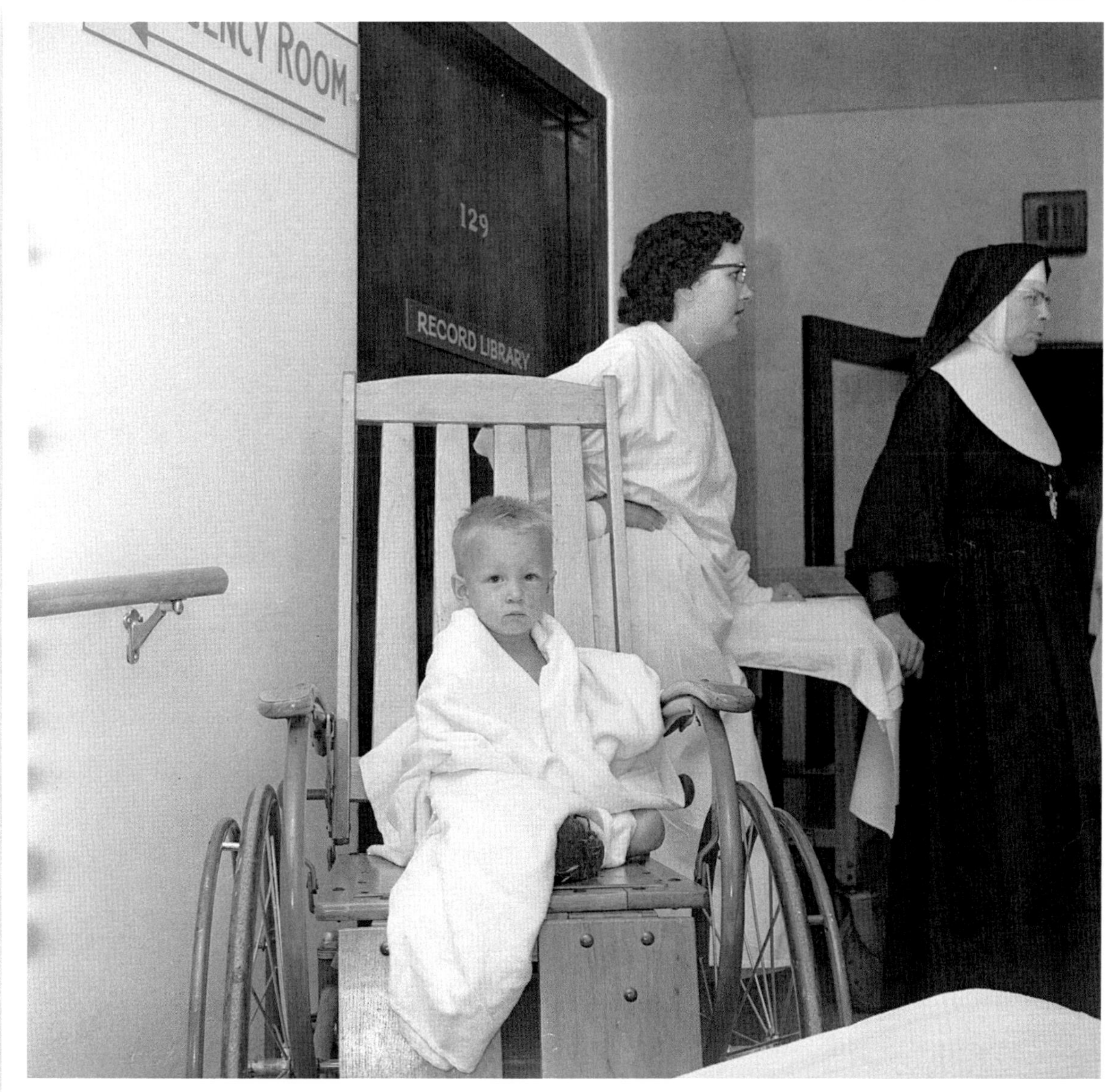

Michael Naylor, 4, in wheelchair at St. John's Hospital, Fargo. Michael's mother, Janet Naylor, was a nurse at St. John's. (NDSU Institute for Regional Studies)

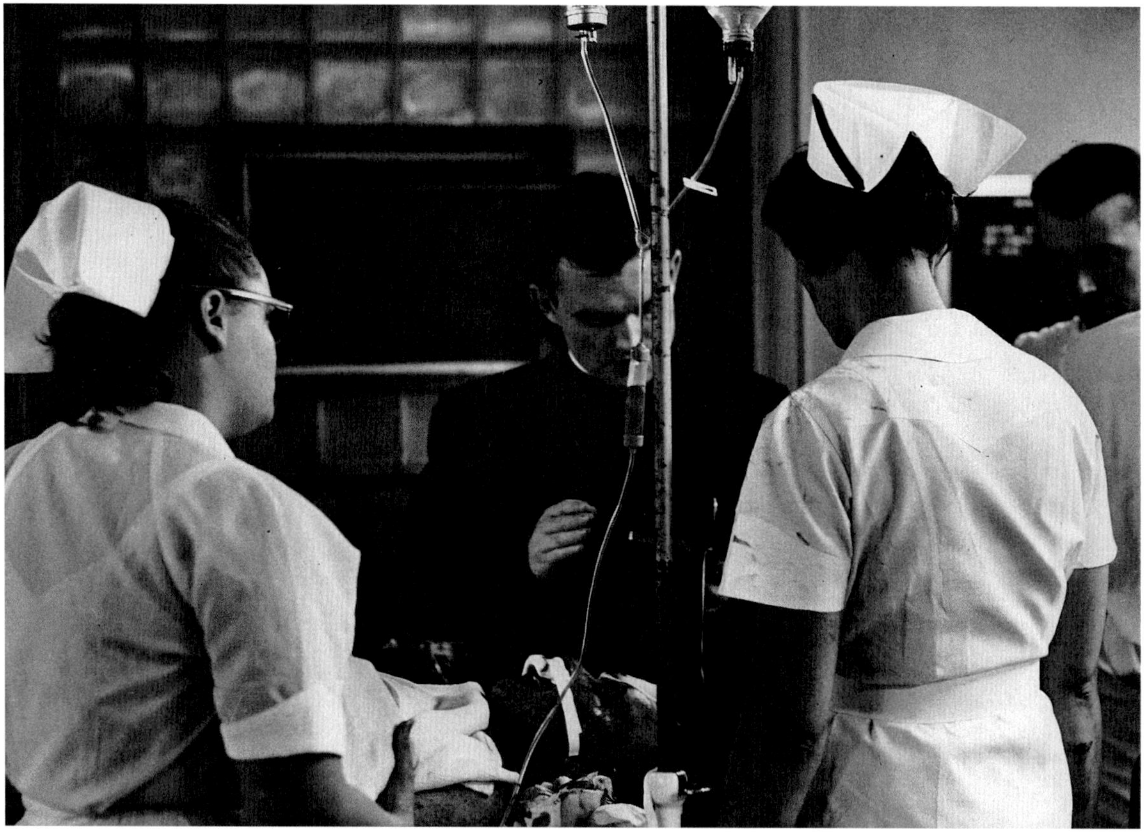

Fr. William Sherman, a priest at St. Mary's Cathedral in Fargo, administers Last Rites at St. Luke's Hospital in Fargo. Fr. Sherman later said of the day, "When the tornado struck it truly did sound like a freight train ... By the time I got to the hospital all hell was breaking loose. I was the only clerical person there. One of the gifts of celibacy is that I was able to be available so soon after the disaster. I gave Catholic rites to about 20 people. I'm very happy to report that not one person died at St. Luke's." (the Forum)

The Absolution of the Dead

> "I have seen death; show me the resurrection."
> —Madeline Gleason

Absolve them
of whatever they took with them
into the winds.

Of youthful failings
or the bitter ranting of old age

Of the heady pride
we all exulted in
at twenty-one or thirty
or the stone-set
stubbornness of fifty.

Erase it
as one would erase
the pencil marks
of a drawing.

Erase their unfinished lines
and let what they had
grow beautiful
in your sight
as a dawn does
for us who sit up
all night
waiting for it.

(NDSU Institute for Regional Studies)

That sweet other place

> "Death is struck, and nature quaking,
> All creation is awaking."
> —The People's Anglican Missal

What do I, priest and poet,
know of the kind of mourning those
who knew them better
managed?

My training limits me.
I can write, or I can pray.
I can take them—
their names written neatly
on cardstock marked with an ancient symbol
from some ancient catacomb—
and offer it upon the fair linen.
I can set it there
and intone absolutions for them—
erasing from them
what everyone else has forgotten.

That is all I can do.
Only I, and other priests, can absolve.
Only we can join our hands
thumb to thumb
or outstretched in a tight *orans*
and make right what lay unfinished.

We set the incense—
blessed with a special collect
I learned one hot afternoon
at seminary—

into the air and watch its smoke
as it snakes and curls upward
into a ghostly pillar
over the list of names
we pronounce now
like a litany of saints
praying for us—
often in vain—
in that sweet other place.

Afterword

Lux Perpetua

"Lux Perpetua
By such glimmer we seek you."

—George Mackay Brown

Relics

for Lynn Brown
(Betty and Don's daughter)

"This is all there is," she says as
she carefully lays out what she has.
"Not much survived the tornado—
only whatever Mom and Dad gave to others.
Whatever they had was blown away or destroyed."

And there they lay—
the last relics of what remained.
Newspapers, yellowing and crisp, wrapped in plastic.
Two plastic-covered funeral home books,
each containing typewritten service information
and the wasted signatures of mostly now-long-dead relatives
who came in hats and gloves
to stand around awkwardly,
unable to do more than to politely sign the book
and to imitate each other's postures of mourning.

Later she showed me the endtable her father made,
a photo of her mother with her sister Kathie Jo the previous Christmas,
a letter Betty wrote dated April 17, 1957—
the handwriting looking so incredibly like my mother's I go breathless—
signed "Love, Betty, Don & the girls."

And finally, his wallet—
a simple, stitched-together brown leather
with hand-tooled diamond-shapes and typical 1950s designs.
And the small pile of its contents—
a drivers license set to expire on June 30, 1957,
his signature in smeared blue ink, a fishing license,
an employee pass last dated "6-19-57,"

all of it water-warped and smeared with traces of mud.
I held them carefully, as though touching brittle bone,
realizing with astonishment:
all this went up with him into the winds.
All this came down and lay there with him
in that place they found him.

We sit here, across the kitchen table from each other,
the relics of the lives of parents she never knew and has no memory of,
lying before us like the slaughtered femurs of martyrs.
They seem almost too sacred to touch.
Rather, they should be gathered up and placed
not back in shoe boxes and zip-lock bags
but under altar stones and in reliquaries.

"It's funny," she finally says after our silences.
"As a little girl, they would tell me about her and her coma,
about how she would open her eyes whenever
anyone would enter the room,
and how she just never really focused.
It's strange but…"

She pauses.

"I guess, back then, I always thought she opened her eyes
because she was waiting for my dad.
I really believed she was waiting for him to come for her."

She stops and swallows hard.

"She held on, fighting, waiting for him for to come to her.
And then…"

"And then, he finally did," I said.

We sit here, looking down at these scattered pieces
of another time, of two achingly young lives
we are barely able to trace,
to document and to say,
with any real conviction,
"they were."

She looks up then and smiles and says,
"I guess it's silly and sentimental isn't it,
to think that way?"

"Not at all," I say.

As I get up and we part,
as I walk into the oppressively hot June afternoon to my car
I really can imagine it—
not that other June evening
when everything turned black with clouds and wind
but rather that cold January day,
when she opened her eyes and focused,
and heard those words she,
in that lingering, seemingly eternal purgatory,
longed to hear.

"Come," I imagine him saying to her.
"It's time. Let's go."

And together, they do.

Tornado memorial at Madison Elementary School, Golden Ridge in Fargo. (photo by author)

Notes

Intro: Mechtild of Magdeburg (1210-c.1280) German Cistercian nun and mystic.

Opening quotes: Elizabeth Bishop (1911-1979), American poet; Rusty Draper (1923-2003) was an American popular music singer; Elizabeth Cotton (1895-1987), American folk musician. She supposedly wrote "Freight Train" in her early teens while watching a freight train passing her house on Lloyd Street in Carrboro, North Carolina.

"It approaches...": Edwin Denby (1903-1983), American poet.

"From there": Judith Wright (1915-2000), Australian poet.

"Every day": Joel Oppenheimer (1930-1988), American poet; Olav H. Hauge (1908-1994), Norwegian poet.

"Betty&Don": Henry Vaughan (1621-1695), English Metaphysical poet and Anglican priest.

"A brighter morrow": The hymn "Praise God, this hour of sorrow," written by the German poet and hymn-writer Johann Heermann (1585-1647), is from *The Lutheran Hymnary,* copyright 1913, 1935. Augsburg Publishing.

"O Salutaris": "O salutaris Hostia/ Quae caeli pandis ostium" is Latin for "O salutary Victim/ Who expands the door of the sky"; from a hymn written by St. Thomas Aquinas (1225-1274); The Brass Rail was a bar located at 816 Front Street (now Main Avenue) in Fargo. *Gunfight at the O.K. Corral* (1957) was a film starring Burt Lancaster as Wyatt Earp and Kirk Douglas as Doc Holliday; The Fargo Theatre was (and is still) located on Broadway in Fargo.

"Her Prayer": Kadya Molodowsky (1894-1975), Lithuanian-born, American Yiddish poet.

"Finding Him": The collect ending "Mercifully grant..." is from *The Common Service Book of the Lutheran Church,* copyright 1917, 1918, The United Lutheran Church in America; *"Ipsis, Domine, et omnibus in Christo..."* is a prayer from the "Commemoration of the Dead" from the Roman Canon of the Mass. It is translated as: "To these, O Lord, and to all that rest in Christ, grant, we beseech Thee, a place of refreshment, light, and peace; Through the same Christ our Lord. Amen."

"The Wind, One Dusk": Antonio Machado (1875-1939), Spanish poet.

Agha Shahid Ali (1949-2001) American poet.

"After the Storm": Marianne Moore (1887–1973) American poet.

"These hands": Luis Buñuel (1900-1983) Spanish-Mexican film-maker; Herschel Lashkowitz (1918-1993), Mayor of Fargo from 1954 to 1974; Richard Hugo (1923-1982) American poet.

"The Wind Will Take it": Marguerite de Navarre (1492–1549) was the queen consort of King Henry II of Navarre, as well as a poet and author, and was referred to as "The First Modern Woman."

"Mercedes": Miguel Hernandez (1910-1942) Spanish poet.

"Ghostly": Walter Hilton (1340-1396) English Augustinian mystic.

"Agnus Dei": R.S. Thomas (1913-2000) Welsh poet and Anglican priest.

"The Absolution of the Dead": Madeline Gleason (1903-1979) American poet, born in Fargo.

"Afterward: Lux Perpetua": George Mackay Brown (1921-1996) Scottish poet.

About the Press

North Dakota State University Press (NDSU Press) exists to stimulate and coordinate interdisciplinary regional scholarship. These regions include the Red River Valley, the state of North Dakota, the plains of North America (comprising both the Great Plains of the United States and the prairies of Canada), and comparable regions of other continents. We publish peer reviewed regional scholarship shaped by national and international events and comparative studies.

Neither topic nor discipline limits the scope of NDSU Press publications. We consider manuscripts in any field of learning. We define our scope, however, by a regional focus in accord with the press's mission. Generally, works published by NDSU Press address regional life directly, as the subject of study. Such works contribute to scholarly knowledge of region (that is, discovery of new knowledge) or to public consciousness of region (that is, dissemination of information, or interpretation of regional experience). Where regions abroad are treated, either for comparison or because of ties to those North American regions of primary concern to the press, the linkages are made plain. For nearly three-quarters of a century, NDSU Press has published substantial trade books, but the line of publications is not limited to that genre. We also publish textbooks (at any level), reference books, anthologies, reprints, papers, proceedings, and monographs. The press also considers works of poetry or fiction, provided they are established regional classics or they promise to assume landmark or reference status for the region. We select biographical or autobiographical works carefully for their prospective contribution to regional knowledge and culture. All publications, in whatever genre, are of such quality and substance as to embellish the imprint of NDSU Press.

We changed our imprint to North Dakota State University Press in January 2016. Prior to that, and since 1950, we published as the North Dakota Institute for Regional Studies Press. We continue to operate under the umbrella of the North Dakota Institute for Regional Studies, located at North Dakota State University.